STAMPEDE

and the

Westness of West

STAMPEDE

and the
Westness of West

for Wayne + Kim

Aritha van Herk

at last !

Aritha ~ Herk

ih Frontenac House

Calgary, Alberta

Book design: Neil Petrunia, Epix Design
Cover Image: Burce Selyem
Author photo: Trudie Lee

Library and Archives Canada Cataloguing in Publication

Van Herk, Aritha, 1954-, author
     Stampede and the westness of west / Aritha van Herk.

Poems.
Issued in print and electronic formats.
ISBN 978-1-927823-49-1 (paperback).–ISBN 978-1-927823-50-7
(pdf).–ISBN 978-1-927823-51-4 (html)

     1. Calgary Stampede–Poetry. I. Title.

PS8593.A545S73 2016   C811'.54   C2016-901960-8
                                                C2016-901961-6

Frontenac House gratefully acknowledges the support of the Canada Council for the Arts for our
publishing program. We would also like to thank the Government of Alberta Multimedia Development
Fund for their support of our publishing program.

Canada Council   Conseil des Arts
for the Arts   du Canada   Alberta▮ Government

Printed and bound in Canada
Published by Frontenac House Ltd.
1648 Bowness Road NW
Calgary, Alberta, T2N 3J9, Canada
Tel: 403-263-7025

for Vanja Polić Jurković,
Zagreb cowgirl extraordinaire

Contents

Acknowledgements

I owe tremendous gratitude to the Calgary Stampede and their incredible staff and volunteers, whose generous support gave me insights into this exceptional event. I was their Artist-in-Residence in the year Calgary was the Cultural Capital of Canada, 2012.

Thank you to the Glenbow Archives for their kind assistance and their stewardship of western materials, especially Guy Weadick's correspondence.

Thank you to the Banff Centre's Leighton Colony, which gave me time and space to write.

Thank you to Harry Sanders and Brian Stanko for their research, friendship, and encouragement.

Thank you to Brian Rusted, Lynette Loeppky, Carolynn Hoy, and the smart, talented, and beautiful Unmentionables. You know who you are. And to Jackie Flanagan, who reads with a Calgary eye.

Thank you to Peter and Anita and the little blue house with the enigmatic ghost.

Profound thanks to Frontenac House, for their dedication to good writing and beautiful books.

My love to Robert Sharp, as enthusiastic and engaged a partner as any Stampeding woman could want.

A different version of "Fence/lines" was part of the The McIntyre Ranch Project Exhibition, July 29 - September 11, 2005, Southern Alberta Art Gallery, Lethbridge, Alberta. It was first published in the Calgary Stampede's *Western Art Show Catalogue*. Calgary, Alberta: 2006.

A different version of "Shooting a Saskatoon" was first published in *Challenging Frontiers*. Ed. Lorry Felske and Beverly Rasporich. Calgary: University of Calgary Press, 2004. It was first performed, by Aritha van Herk and Brian Stanko, at Banff, October, 1998.

The lines from Robert Kroetsch are in *Completed Field Notes*. Toronto: McClelland and Stewart, 1989.

The dreaming

On the pages of winter, horses gallop through the darkness that is our heirloom, here on the grasslands bent and whispering under the hibernating season.

Invisible, those ghost hooves raise the dust of summer, the sweetness of heat, while thunderclouds stockpile the fervor of broil.

A snowstorm tempts us to remember July, its sweltering grandstand thick with beer and cotton candy, blurred clamor of the announcer through a babel sound system, the cries of hucksters, the stripe of fireworks.

Stampede coming. A certain anniversary that will arrive despite resistance or annoyance, despite the strange thrum of "until." Not tomorrow, but always in the seventh month, the off-centre pivot of the year turning on its axis, saturnalia biding its time.

Who counts the days to Stampede? Caterers, accountants, special events coordinators, straw bales, beer bottles, window painters.

And who leaves town? The curled lip, the shoulder-shrug dismissing this déclassé debauch, this faux fiesta, with its ragbag history and bricolage of excess. The sniffy contempt: primitive. As if that were an insult. Some say you're not a true Calgarian until you leave town to avoid the Stampede.

Let's admit it. Joy gets no respect. Popular jubilation and unfettered diversion are suspect, not to be trusted. Never indulge the instability of the mob, its desire to kick the traces, massing the streets in that social deformity known as fun.

Am I trapped in a synthetic documentary? Do I breathe a brief trace of what Stampede might have been or what we will remember tomorrow? Am I artist or patron? Or just someone practising disguise?

Is this the west then, legend or performance, the old west, the new west, the wild west, the faint west, the dusty west, the wicked west, the uncultivated west, the dishevelled west, the tempestuous west, the unkempt west, the turbulent west, the tousled west, the complaining west, the anarchic west, the restless west, windswept, rumpled and unironed and messy, its depiction as wildly unpredictable as its chaotic generation, a shambles and a jumble and a pandemonium of hope.

Stampede or else.

The infield

Showdown hovers at the fringe of the arena, the infield sand ready to soak up blood or rain or sweat, rancor and rivalry beside the Elbow River's mosquito rocky banks.

In the combed dirt of the ring, cowboys and horses pretend this tournament is not theatrical, a choreographed dance with fortune and possibility, a roster of rules, a wager of prediction, a struggle between balance and bruises.

Hazard the probability. A chance to slip in blood, a chance to claim injury, a chance to bite the dust. Gambling the true sport for those who would court thoracic compression, strained biceps, torn posterior cruciate ligaments, C2 fractures, and sheer terror.

What competition suggests an outcome better than a clock? An eight-second clock, impossibly short and impossibly long.

Measure that scarce commodity, the human attention span. Just enough time to cross the hedgehog chasm, but not enough to charm a goldfish.

Eight seconds:
> eight seconds to count down
> eight seconds to lose a hat
> eight seconds to watch and wait
> eight seconds to lurch into the past
> eight seconds to see a life flash forward
> eight seconds after the gate swings open, that gap into infinity

Ride at your own risk. Assent to danger.

Joy before death.

It takes:

> eight seconds to answer a phone
> eight seconds to form an impression
> eight seconds to fall in love at first sight
> eight seconds to solve a puzzle
> eight seconds for an average sound bite
> eight seconds to zip a fly

A long wait.

Think of eight seconds on the back of a plunging bronc.

An eternity. Eight seconds is a long, long time.

Somebody's got to know when to stop.

Anticipation

Stampede on its way. A rush, a flight, a charge, headlong.

This bacchanal, the spirit of summer hovering past the reach of the lilac blooming hedge, the rains of June, the tenderfoot tradition.

Some mélange of economic impact, hoot and holler, wild ride, the outcome when many large animals or people hasten in the same direction.

Causes of stampede:
    fear
    being spooked
    laziness
    panic
    flight
    a misdirection of direction

Don't frighten the horses, try not to frighten the people, intimidate the fences, the ticket booths, the damnable moneychangers and palm-readers, those sellers of carpet steamers and massage chairs.

Thirst:
    anticipation
    whiskey
    arousal
    dehydration

Polydipsia, the inverse of the dipsomaniacs we all become. The tang of a charge, careering toward light and dust, the open sweep of hills hanging there to the west, a watchful bluff of surmise.

Cattle are slow to respond. They submit to judging grudgingly, recalcitrant or ruminant as their broad foreheads, their brisket chests. Shouts, arm-waving, a stinging lasso; their own bovine temperament, their muzzles a mood. Lightning bolts can move them, but not necessarily. Until they do. Stampede, that is.

Three parts to Stampede:
    horses
    cattle
    people

Add fire; thunderstorms; late dawns, hungover and incurable, to remedy the dog end of night. That self-inflicted dolorosa. Stranger than dust.

Cipher boots and snap-button shirts, the brag of a buckle.

Mix in a tub of beer bottles, the hot reek of sausage rolling on a grill.

Stage a roundup. Pretend it can happen in a big city, crowded enough to claim metropolis. Herd together the drinkers and grifters, the real estate salesmen and petro engineers, the impresarios and party planners. One massive pub crawl. This impulse run, this bottled adversary.

Pretend to the insight of *Homo Ludens,* the play of culture with its erotic dalliance and games of chance, its jocular delight and dancing masks of death.

Playing around and playing along.

Playing fast and loose.

Waiting for the rodeo.

Ranch hands

Canadian Cattlemen gives advice: "Take a beetle-headed bronc, saddle it, go out on the range and do a day's work on it and eventually teach the horse something worth while."

Cowboys now answer to ranch hands, but the old name sticks to their homesickness, the bristle of buckle and hat impossible to escape.

"Cowboy" has kicked around for centuries. A term imported from England. First appeared in 1725, courtesy of Jonathan Swift, no less, in "A Receipt to Restore Stella's Youth," where the Irish parodist extols the virtues of beef and wine, mirth, exercise and fresh air. He might have been working for the Stampede. Maybe he still does.

There gallops the myth, in the naming, onomastic.

Movies and fiction, games and kisses.

Cattleman, cowhand, rancher. Nothing so exotic as gaucho or vaquero.

These cowpunchers drive pick-ups, wear trainers, dress down for dinner. Might agree to a leather jacket, a bolo tie on a special occasion.

They shoot from the shoulder.

They doff their hats to Roethke.

They remember not the taming of Bucephalus, but the placid canter of what was once the undertaker's horse, its hideously suggestive professional pace down a street stilled by ceremony, heads bowed. The hearse cometh.

But the dream persists.

Cowboys yearn not for activists and bikini models but for the tomboy cousin who understands what a crownpiece does. She knows how to slip a bridle over a nose without spooking the horse. She is the one who whispers instead of shrieking. Stoic, sturdy enough to cull a calf from the herd and hold it down for vaccination and castration.

Long live cowboys.

Save a horse, ride a cowboy, har, har, it's a bumpy commute.

Their thick Kevlar vests, their strong necks and sweet faces, the set of their ears under that parable.

Where do cowboys come from? Airdrie and Dorothy, Rosebud and High River.

That thrust of the hip, the truculent chin, arms akimbo. And the squinting, shaded eyes.

Busted up, most of them, a hobble or limp evidence of experience, a collection of trophy hangovers.

Give me a purty cowboy, one who sits straight up in the saddle, rides a long stirrup, and tops off a bucking horse with ease.

Then I'll pony up.

Parade in a snowstorm

Pray for sunshine. Expect downpour.

Calgary weather, truculent and fickle:
  high winds
  rain
  more rain
  potential floods
  past floods
  early blizzards
  late blizzards
  summer blizzards
  heavy rain
  light rain
  wind gusts
  thunderstorms
  lightning
  heavy winds
  hail
  blizzard

Get out the parka – it's parade day.

Banners barely visible, clotted with summer snow.

The horns sound adenoidal and the tubas have sore throats. Xylophones convert to snow shovels.

Harry the Horse slouches along the route, not mascot but prisoner.

The parade parades, rain or shine.

Umbrellas ride shoulders and hat brims droop under the weight of moisture.

Horseshoes muffle the slush.

Faint yahoos for the miniature donkeys plowing through wet snow up to their miniature knees. Beer-wagon Clydesdales, spitting llamas. Ponies with ribbons braided into their manes.

The clowns' makeup runs, real tears mixing with painted.

The curb regulars festoon their lawn chairs with plastic covers, stake out their annual spot. Riding the roof edges are the office workers with the bird's eye view. Can't see through the flurries. Tipping their coffee cups up to cool their watch.

Stampede snowfall.

Noise

What storm will thunder the arena?

The accelerated heartbeat of waiting.

The thump of music, country music with a rocky edge. Even scornful hipsters become secret country music fans.

The shaking ground, the barrage of fireworks, the heartless cheers of the crowd.

Noises not off but point blank.

Uproar and thud.

Detonation and din.

Ordinary horses

Buck and Punch and Sally, Stryder and Ranger. Danny.

Now forgotten, horses carried off to the knackers, but once horses of the night, imperious.

The Prince of Wales' horses were named Drizzle and Blue Sky. Steel Grey lived farther south.

Joey was the racehorse whose shoes were auctioned at a Victory Bond rally for $40,000.

We had a horse on the farm. Pocahontas, we called her. Recalcitrant, stubborn, her own determined beast. Snorted every time we came close. She made us fear her bolt, the nervous toss of her head.

We didn't dare to ride our horse; she was decorative, black and fat and disrespectful. She had found herself a retirement pasture. Refused to be ridden. Chased the cows when she took a mind to confuse them.

My father bought her at auction. Saved her from the slaughterhouse. He backed the wrong horse, although he could ride her. We couldn't and she knew it.

Bravery at issue.

I put a saddle on a sawhorse and tried to make it buck. It was immobile. I wasn't about to become a bronc-rider.

Today, I rest a door across a sawhorse for a desk.

Horse town

"Think, when we talk of horses, that you see them
Printing their proud hoofs i' the receiving earth."
  ~ *Henry V,* Prologue

The First Peoples called Calgary "horse town" because the settlement was a social hub for horses. Horses outnumbered people. Stables and barns were more important than bars, and hay the most important fuel, straw a necessary resource. Horses dragged fire wagons, laundry vans, milk carts, sleighs, a hearse or two, buggies and rigs, carriages and apple-carts.

Saddle and blinders, halters and bridles. And as for stirrups, useful footrests, contentious as history, the People could take or leave them, use them or not, their ease on the backs of horses audacious. They neither knew nor cared that mouldy scholars would argue deep into the night about medieval technology and the advantages of the stirrup to the spread of feudalism in Europe, doing battle in the Great Stirrup Controversy and its promotion of warfare on horseback.

The People held to horses as a sign of wealth, speed, movement, and beauty.

They've bequeathed the city their reverence. More than a hundred statues of horses scattered through Calgary.

Calgary was started by men on horses, surreptitiously covering indiscretion with their uniforms, drinking the whiskey they confiscated. The NWMP rode in, dragging their mounts, determined to be heroic. Almost succeeding. Stepped off their horses' backs at the confluence of the Bow and the Elbow, relieved to leave the stirrups. Tough paints survived that trek, but fine Ontario thoroughbreds died along the way.

Local horses rule. Horses are our icons, a declaration that we are still historical. We stare into the eye of the horse, celebrate the year of the horse. ·

Herbivorous quadruped: Old English, from *khursa,* old norse. That kind of pedigree, connected to the Latin of *currere,* to run, another form of education.

Horses have inspired centuries of statues and paintings, drawings and bronzes.

Ridden by kings and children, queens and generals.

The "Wild Horse" ivory found in the Vogelherd Cave, now captive in Tubingen.

The horses of Dordogne, their sculpted frieze under the Abri du Cap Blanc, and the skeleton of the Magdalenian woman buried at the foot of the great horse.

Bring back the *caballoid,* a way to understand the dense orthography of this creature, renounce or embrace the paleogenomic sequencing of a 700,000-year-old horse metapodial bone from Canada. Pleistocene beyond our comprehension.

Remember Przewalski, aka Przhevalsky, who wanted to get to Tibet's holy city of Lhasa. He took the long way around, through the Gobi Desert, Beijing, up the Yangtze, became a repeat Marco Polo.

Mad with collection, he brought back to Russia 5000 plants, 1000 birds and 3000 insect species, along with animal skins, reptiles, and a bad case of saddle burn, along with problematic taxonomies and a dozen angry lovers.

Searched Mongolia for wild horses, determined to discover if they were real or imaginary. They were real but elusive, the only horses never domesticated.

Given his name, Przewalski, a breed square-headed and stocky and thick-skinned. Their mane bristles erect. They host 66 chromosomes instead of 64 like other horses. Their legs bear the faint stripes of primitive inheritance.

The discovery of the horse:
    a mixture of awe and perturbation
    what kind of animal is this
    does it speak
    will it be ridden

There was once a superstitious taboo against uttering the name of an animal so important, all that ability to prance silenced on the tongue.

Cow town replaced horse town. A safeguard to our talisman.

Visitors

I've taken lovers to the Stampede.

And husbands.

Sisters and brothers.

Cousins from the old country.

Visitors from Croatia and Paris.

Compatriots and clandestines.

Lost small wailing children in the horse barn.

Taken relatives who managed to look patient and puzzled.

Taken clients who politely looked away.

Taken irritating colleagues who asked rude questions.

Taken Edmontonians. Enough said.

Sent enemies when I was certain they would develop hay fever and blisters.

Refused to go when I was grumpy.

Lined up for hours to hear bad country music.

Parade

Nightmare morning for politicians.

No horse, no carriage, no legs.

Lame.

Wagons for wusses.

If you want to be Premier, you have to ride a horse.
If you want to be Prime Minister, you have to ride a horse.
If you want to be Mayor, you have to ride a horse.

Nenshi on horseback: "This horse gets taller every year."

Every Councillor and MLA and MP hefts a flabby butt aloft and mounts.

Disquieting, the strain between the thighs, the witness to public play and potential humiliation. Pray for a parade-broke horse.

Did you see that?
He fell off his horse.
Can't vote for him.

Required: the ability to ride a horse.

No question about that four-legged quadruped and its profanity.

Parade marshalls, dignitaries, princesses, astride
Astronauts, actors, singers, astride
Four-year-olds on broomsticks, astride
Leather jockeys, astride

Lesson for the day: how to get on a horse.

Can't even imagine the act of saddling. Hope someone else has done it, and tightened the cinch properly.

Stand beside the horse. Take a moment to pray, quietly, an instant of faith.

Hope that this is a calm horse, well fed, parade-broke, accustomed to children and skittering creatures, not to mention cunning politicians.

Take the reins in your hand. Hold them firmly, as if you mean it, as if you understand what reins do. Hope that they are instruments of control and not flapping straps of leather that will start a stampede.

The secret to mounting is to gather with the reins a tuft of mane, that tug on the horse's crest enough to remind the creature of human authority. Someone else's authority, not yours.

Which is worse – riding a recalcitrant horse through a hooting hollering crowd, or marching four kilometres, flat-footed, blatting on a tuba over griddle-hot asphalt?

Now what kind of question is that?

Parade. Spectacle and fuss, we are prone to beating that dead horse, its corpse useful as completion. And it is too late to swap horses while crossing this river, although that too is a bad idea, leading to drowning more often than not.

Stand beside this proverbial gift horse, which will elevate you above the crowd and prove you've been elected, but can also turn you into farce, a laughing stock.

The politician at the voter's bar, riding a horse foaled of an acorn, and there "be hanged from the gallows" of spectators and parade Marshalls alike.

The horse knows the route. The horse knows the ropes. The horse is a horse, a horse that knows you do not know horses. And so it snorts, as if to warn you against the danger that you pose to yourself.

Snorting communicates possible danger to other horses.

Got a novice here.

Consult the Equine Behaviorist, smug with answers.

"I hope this helps you to understand what your horse is saying when he snorts."

"I hope this helps you to understand your horse."

That blaze down his face? The mark of a balker.

Smile with all your cheeks. That would be the cheeks of your derriere.

Perhaps the snort is a message: "Stay away. Beware. Not another Stampede parade, how many times do we have to do this? Are you serious?"

Ride this horse at your peril.

There must be another rider, pale or shaded, who will appear, who will rescue you from disgrace.

A prairie woman, fierce and rude, cantering in on horseback.

A woman who can ride is the woman of the hour.

She becomes equestrienne, as enigmatic as her animal. Beware.

The occasion of the parade is to start a stampede.

Start the Stampede.

Parade marshall

Cappy Smart and Cappy Smart and Cappy Smart. Parade Marshall for more than 30 years. Burned the house down. Died two weeks after his last parade, 1939, forcibly retired by his own bereavement. He died.

Even today Cappy Smart's ghost marches at the head of the bands and floats, swinging his arms as if he were still fire chief.

The honour given to others:
  Nancy Greene – skier
  Bing Crosby and Wilf Carter – crooners
  Bob Hope – jokester
  Walt Disney – animator and film producer
      chaperoned by Mickey and Minnie
  Robert Kennedy – south of the border
  Treaty Seven Chiefs – regalia
  Gordie Howe – right winger
  Chris Hadfield – astronaut
  Soldiers and Prime Ministers – in uniform
  Kaillie Humphries – bobsledder
  Iris Glass – matriarch of chuckwagons

Missing marshalls:
  Joe Carbury – "And they'rrrreee offfff"
  George Stanley – maple leaf flag
  Nellie McClung – votes and persons
  W.O. Mitchell – *Who Has Seen* … .

Race

Races too now ghosted and gone.

The thoroughbreds dropped in 1976, racing usurped by rodeo.

No point in Calgary getting on its high horse, every race will be balked by another bust. Affect airs of superiority at our peril.

And horseplay is horseplay, we're happy enough if there is no injury. Not enough at stake to keep racing for racing's sake.

In Siena, Italy, the horses scramble around the Campo at a speed breakneck to history, the medieval *Il Palio* still run twice a year. Tribal, which of the Contrade will be chosen, the intensity of the race repeated and repeated for the favour of the Virgin Mary's gonfalon. Singing and shouting, the horses cosseted and the jockeys bribed, old blood wagers hanging in the air while the social clubs perform street banquets for thousands and the church waves its banners.

Siena cherishes horses, their brilliant sleights, offers up processions and pageantry. These horses are guarded. They bespeak the future.

And the race, vicious pandemonium, a bareback cauldron run around the sloping Campo, ardent with danger, brutal and swift. The corners of the Campo cushioned to protect the horses, but veterinarians lurk with injections at the side streets. Riders whipped and bribed and mocked and urged onwards to their inevitable injuries, colours flying to mute their blood.

No horsing around, no game, but a serious feud between enemy Contrade. And the winning horse ridden into church to be blessed.

An all-out race, and no mere parade, with its weak *Yahoos* and fluttering bandanas. We're a tame country with a tame investment in competition. Barely medieval at all.

The gamble and the measure, which horse is faster on that oval track, that dirt aureole.

The horse's mouth

Let the horse speak immutable truth through its teeth, those same teeth that can inflict serious pain. She's a biter. Don't bend over if you don't want her to nip your derriere.

A girl with long hair was a horse and buggy sort, meaning "old-fashioned," properly moral, and out of date.

Slang for heroin. As opposed to white pony for cocaine. And how is this relevant, we ask ourselves, still standing next to the horse we are doomed to ride, afraid of the hour, the long traipse around a concrete circle.

Horse sense gone off to hibernate, along with the strength of horseradish, although the condiment reappears with beef on a bun, somewhat tamed by its pickling.

We want to find that horseshoe, its promise of luck, escape the horse latitudes with their subtropical highs and unpredictable winds. Puzzled about the "dead horse" ritual of sailors on the high seas, when the straw-stuffed effigy of a horse was paraded around the deck before being thrown overboard to satisfy the gods of debt.

And if there are lists of dead heroes, where are the horses of Achilles and Aeneas and Ajax, Hector and Heracles, Louis Riel and Terry Fox? Grazing in the pastures of buffalo. Lampos and Bayard scorning our short-lived myths.

Stop horsing around.

Pancake banquet

The breakfast shuffle. A queue of weary clerks and landsmen waiting for their servings of pancakes and bacon, some fat to fight the nausea, some carbs to play it forward. A conga file, a column of supplicants salivating for the chew of dough, the sweet melt of syrup and butter under the tyranny of a plastic fork and knife, an inadequate napkin, the buckling paper plate. One sausage for reward.

The day is cooler than correctness.

The line-up shambles politely, too early in the week for the crescive rudeness that will soon set in.

So many pancake mendicants that the batter gets thrown in a cement mixer.

Outside, in a bronze dawn, the morning chill arouses the same ravenous hunger that set Stampede in motion.

Hunger or weary acquiescence?

Flapjacks a metaphor for comfort.

Contents battered.

Stalwart and sturdy. On the Stampede Board.

Pericles, Prince of Tyre, was manifestly corrupt, it's said, but when he washed up on the shore of Pentapolis, he was promised pancakes by the fishermen who rescued him.

Pericles not Shakespeare's play, the critics claim, but some second rate scribble put together by George Wilkins, who was a licensed victualler, panderer, dramatist and pamphleteer, the perfect combination. Best friend of the men who quadrupled the Big Four.

And although the fact is not well-known, victuallers started their own school, which survives to this day, the Licensed Victuallers' School, or LVS Ascot, an independent all-ability school for pupils in the English county of Berkshire.

And nothing to do with learning to cook or providing food to erstwhile travellers.

The Scarlet Letter flips flapjacks:
    pre-heat the skillet
    pay attention
    wield the spatula decisively
    know when to turn that browning hotcake

Pannenkoeken are the Dutch version, my own. Less flour and more liquid, no baking powder. Flour, salt, eggs, milk. Fried in butter in a cast iron pan. Pay attention. The house could burn down. Thin and rollable, with a dusting of butter, sugar and cinnamon.

But Stampede Pancakes are their own creatures, half-raw to burned, browned perfectly or pale at the edges, their serrated circle low-born communion wafer.

Thirty thousand breakfasts.
A thousand gallons of batter.
Thirty-five hundred pounds of bacon.

Breakfast, that bleary meal transformed to ambrosia, flavoured by eating *al fresco,* the hint of rain, the chilly dawn complete with its inevitable arousal into a tough sun.

See also:
    flapcakes
    battercakes
    johnnycakes
    hoe cakes
    flannel cakes
    griddle cakes
    quick bread
    crepes
    tanganites
    hotcakes
    slapjacks

The same pancake that resolved not to be eaten and rolled away, chased by a dozen children, and eventually gobbled down by an intelligent pig, who had no intention of declaring his intentions. And ate the pancake.

Thomas Jefferson loved pancakes, sent French chef Etienne Lemaire's recipe for *panne-quaiques,* the crepe version, home to Monticello.

Literary too. Nathanial Hawthorne, when he was first married, addressed pancakes at great length, how good they were, piping hot, the emblem of his largess when George Hillard and his wife came from Boston to visit the old Manse at Concord, Massachusetts. Hawthorne treated them to "a splendid breakfast of flapjacks, or slapjacks, and whortleberries, which I gathered on a neighbouring hill."

It is not clear if Sophia Peabody or some kitchen maid cooked those pancakes, but they were flapjacks of the finest order and they made Nathanial Hawthorne – he of *The Scarlet Letter,* a most unhappy morality tale – intensely happy. For once.

Serve immediately.

But never for wedding breakfasts.

Shrove. A practical way to use up perishable ingredients before Lent: eggs, milk, and butter forbidden in the season of abstinence. Examine the sins of the year, count them out and measure them up.

Pancake Day pagan. The change of seasons a struggle between springtime and the sinister forces of cold and darkness, the key to Shrovetide week eating hot, round pancakes, symbols of the light and warmth of the sun.

Shriven. The morning after the night before. Stack 'em up. Sins too.

And back to the origin of that flat cake, made from batter and fried, tasty or not, burned or beautifully brown. The Greeks ate them with honey; the Elizabethans with sherry and apples.

Flat as a pancake, the plains of Canada. A misnomer. The prairie is not flat, but rife with relief.

Flat as a rueful, flat-chested woman. But contradictorily, she's the one who wins the race, flat-out speed. The barrel racer, that is. Remember the way she sits in the saddle. She'll kick any pancake's butt.

Best eaten with whiskey-spiked maple syrup.

Dog trials

World stock dog competition, the smile on the dog's muzzle, only two dogs per handler and the goal penning the sheep, no substitutions.

That low-to-the-ground liquid snake against a wall of wool, sheep stupider than tourists and twice as grumpy, refusing to herd, standing their ground. It is all a dog can do to refrain from biting their ludicrous noses, from nipping at their obtuse heels.

The announcer loves to declare "It's a tough year for sheep," if they're recalcitrant. Always recalcitrant.

The heroes of huddle:
    Tug and Rex
    Heart and Bella
    Jaff and Meg
    Ezra and Crush
    Oreo and Slick
    Amber and Ivy
    Bailey and Bandit
    Jack and Tex

Repeat winners. It's all in the name.

I'll come back in my next life as a border collie with only one job: to get the damn sheep into the pen.

Queens and princesses

Queens of hearts and horses.

The names give them away:
    Kari and Halley
    Patsy and Dawn
    Christie and Tara

Beautiful women who cut and run, who know the business end of a quirt,
who recognize a lazy pair of dungarees when they see them. Who can cook
a steak on their thighs, balance an official on one elbow, remember that
secret recipe for baked beans with bourbon. Who can shear sheep, braid
hair, put on mascara without a smudge.

Interdictions for Stampede Royalty:
    no husbands
    no children
    no sawhorses
    no hip flasks
    no dropouts
    no arrests or accusations

Not younger than 19 and not older than 24.
Never divorced, separated or married.
Not allowed to marry while in office.

The five-year sweet spot.
Does a married woman ride less well?
Does a married woman refuse to be a queen, give up all rights to royalty?

The pre-requisites:
    citizenship and residency
    security check
    living within a 40-mile radius of Calgary
    a driver's license and a truck
        (a big truck with a big bottom and big old wheels)

License:

> in possession of only a horse and a truck
> no impediments
> have wheels, will travel
> have hooves, will amble

And riding ability.

Ride, and ride well, with aplomb and speed, back straight and hands above the pummel.

Ha. Pretty horses and fast women. Their comic refrain, sung to the tune of *Bonanza's* theme music:

> get it up
> get it in
> get it out
> don't mess my hairdo

No swimsuit contests, these women polish off weeks of riding competitions. Ease on the back of a horse, or no crown. Those who ride badly are eliminated, can't afford to have the queen falling off her horse during the grand entry, queens have to dismount voluntarily.

But they are the metaphor, for the queens of the midway, queens of the night, queens on the happy streets of Victoria Park.

Chucks

They start out easy, but as the week tightens, the race gets meaner, the corners of the wagons closer and closer in the turnout around the barrels of the infield.

They chase themselves, those wagons, the thunder of hooves a drum from the past, racing from campsite to saloon, bags of flour sifting white and beans leaping in their bins.

The outriders break for the slipstream, and the creaking mess wagons careen from cooking to confusion. Pile-up inevitable.

Wildhorse Jack would snort and think them tame. He hooked unbroken horses to his wagon, pulled on their tails to make them run faster, swore and screamed, lit firecrackers and dynamite to improve their speed. That's history.

Chuckwagon circuit, that turmoil of chaos, the wild turn around the barrels, and the potential for damage and spills.

Chucks, invented by the Stampede, or at least officially anointed. A sure-fire way to risk horses and men, a guarantee for dust and broken bones, a few fatal pileups.

Confounded confusion. The camp cook as heller.

Ban:
>   whips
>   dynamite
>   shrill whistles
>   the knacker's conclusion
>   a starting gun

Ban the howls of spectators and protesters.

Weadick's promotional literature: "Primitive, rattling, lumbering range-scarred mess wagons fully equipped with flour bags and cast iron frying pans."

Drivers smashing their butt bones on the hard bench, handling the heavy ribbons of reins on the fastest team they can hook together without the horses kicking each other to death. No fear, no flight, the mad adrenalin of the Roman chariot races, too much enthusiasm to ever stop this dancing and its companion copulations.

Now it's the Rangeland Derby.

Lead man and stove man, outriders and driver.

This is called a team, legs pumping together, the smell of victory.

Chuckwagon racing too complex for the ordinary spectator, too sophisticated and intricate.

The most purely Canadian sport. Nobody else does it.

Tradition dies hard:
    every year horses will die
    every year horses will stretch their noses toward Nirvana
    every year, the chuckwagon races will declare themselves *sui generis*
    every year, wagon racing the *ne plus ultra* of Stampede

The grandstand on its feet and screaming at the finish.

And if you don't like it, alas, too bad, *tough shit.*

The missing day

Stampede kidnaps us, bushwhacks us, persuades us that we can fall in love with the belts and the buckles and the snap button shirts.

Laundry every second day, no underwear left, sunburn on the shoulders, and a headache from the hat.

Take the mickey. Forget water.

Find a hay bale to stretch out on.

It's easy to dress western. Too-tight jeans and a plaid shirt, bandana and straw hat. Silver jewellery and a pair of boots, scuffed boots that have lasted ten years.

Recycle that costume every year, change up the jeans once they rip, buy another shirt when the reek of beer and sweat gets the upper hand.

Heavy

Monday head on shoulders.

How to lift that ache and get down the road to work?

Drink six glasses of water and hit the pillow again, who cares, no one takes attendance during Stampede. Can't get fired during Stampede. Can't make a deal during Stampede.

The heavy horse pull, agricultural retro for horses straining stumps out of the ground, heaving buildings to their feet.

A competition where teams of horses drag weights across an arena floor.

Lightweight, middleweight and heavyweight, the heavyweight horse teams weighing a combined 4,466 pounds.

The record: 13,400 pounds, the heaviest weight ever officially recorded.

Jesse and Sam, Doc and Jim, these are the horses you want to marry.

Steady and reliable, they respond to commands, do what they're told.

History

Where does Stampede come from, history and its bones rattling down the road? It's the old pretending to be new and the new pretending to be old.

Eccentric as grass itself, grown tangled in its own roots, the strange kingdom of these rituals.

Pilgrimage and carnival, the waiting and the hurry.

Best-dressed cow and best-dressed cowgirl, the shank of leather between them.

Best-dressed baby, the fattest and the strongest. Three entrants, and the judges gave every mother a prize for fear of maternal fury.

All imitation and adoption, the way that memory makes memory bigger and better.

Guy Weadick went to Paris, took his horse up three elevators to the top of the Tour Eiffel, won a duel with a barber, and bought *vins fins* for ten centimes. His horse was perky but his face looked sad, as if the continent did not agree with him.

Eddie King rode his horse into the Club Café on Stephen Avenue in 1923.

Now someone will take a horse to the top of the Calgary Tower at the beginning of Stampede.

But the grand Buffalo Barbecue was too generous, and has gone extinct.

Wildhorse Jack used up the campstoves and the smoke and the dynamite.

History's antiquity.

Second wind

Catching it. Breathless.

Hurry up please, we're only half-way there, got to find that new burst of energy, the stamina to get through to the 11th day, the day when the dust settles, when the rain comes, when the party is over.

Timing, like death, changes what precedes it.

Buy a new hat, a new pair of boots. Change your shirt, try a new bra combining skimpy with cast iron support. Tuck your phone into the bra, your credit card into its holster.

Get ready for the visit, the repartee, the thorn of lust.

STD tests complimentary. Free-standing clinics.

Nothing left over but sore feet and yearning.

Horse women

Weadick answered queries about the rules.

To Miss Fannie E. Sperry, Mitchell, Montana, who wants to "be in the money in the Ladies Busting Contest."

July 11, 1912:

"We are allowing swell forks saddles provided the swell is not over 15 inches in width. We are also allowing in the ladies contest, the contestants to hobble their stirrups if they so desire. We furnish the bucking horses to all contestants both Ladies and cowboys … .

"The wild horse race is open to the cowboys only, and I would not advise any lady to participate in this particular event as it is rough enough for the men let alone for Ladies."

Who the hell ever told you I was a lady? Split skirts or not.

Tilly Baldwin. Trick rider and relay racer. First woman bulldogger. Her picture on the gold bands around Let'er Buck cigars. Born Anna Matilda Winger, a Norwegian girl who could ski, skate and canoe. She immigrated to New York City at 18, speaking no English, lived with her aunt and became a hairdresser. On an outing to Staten Island she saw some Hollywood cowgirls practising trick riding, and glimpsed her future. She learned to ride, taught herself cowgirl tricks, became a female rodeo star "bulldogging a huge black walleyed steer in fearless fashion." She rode No Sir to a standstill. Was a champion of the Roman Standing race, contestants riding two horses, one foot on each mount. Keep those horses neck and neck. It would frighten most men to death. Chances of falling: higher than average. After that, marriage was a bore.

Bertha Kaepernik Blancett. First woman to ride broncs at Cheyenne. Cried for Cyclone when Tom Three Persons rode Cyclone to a standstill. The only one to enter all the women's events at Calgary in 1912, won the relay race and placed in the others. Took home $1,100 in prize money. A teacher's salary in 1912 was just a bit more than $500. Filed for divorce from Del Blancett on the grounds of desertion when he went off to war. He was killed at Chateau-Thierry on the western front before the divorce went through. Made her madder than before.

Fanny Sperry. Drew Red Wing, who had stomped Joe LaMar to death just a few days before the Stampede started. Rode him to a standstill. *Lady Bucking-Horse Champion of the World.* Never hobbled her stirrups. She could shoot cigars out of her husband's mouth from the back of a galloping horse.

Lucille Mulhall grew up on a ranch in Oklahoma territory, didn't give a damn about territory, first woman to compete against men in roping and riding. Unhesitating. Cowgirl: cow woman, toughie, bossy, brusque. Roosevelt called her a "cowgirl" and the name fastened. 1912 *Champion Lady Steer Roper of the World.* Came to the Stampede to test the border.

Goldie St. Clair rode bucking horses supine, but hurt herself in the Stampede and came in second.

Flores LaDue learned roping tricks before she could walk. Could do the Texas Skip blindfolded. Hang from her horse upside down and rope anything moving or motionless. *Champion Trick Roper.* Narrowly beat Lucille Mulhall. Married to Weadick. Enough said.

"Cowgirls Bucking Horse" and "Cowgirls Relay Race" and "Cowgirls Fancy Roping" a matter of course.

They all won against cowboys.

Now women are illegal, reduced to barrel racers.

Except Linda One Spot, who passed for a boy, in the boys' Wild Steer Riding competition in 1952. Took them a while to figure it out. She was winning.

Girls who ride horses have better posture than those who don't.

Girls who ride horses have long long legs.

Girls who ride horses may be flat-chested, not too much bounce in their bounce.

And as for the "first white woman in the west," what does that category measure? That she was there before they were, but not there at all, a ranch wife scrubbing clothes on a board instead of going to the parade. She would have had a few words for the dust that sifted over her clean lines of laundry, for the all-male board of directors, for the hours of volunteering without making the roster of the organization.

Or having any say.

Buck

Bucking always contentious.

"We have improved our horses out of these habits, and we should be ashamed of them."

Winter free range, and then preparation. Moved from grass to oats, from freedom to exercise. In training.

This is the job of bucking for horses:
15 times a year
eight seconds per buck
120 seconds total
two minutes per summer

Done.

Bucking used to be a ride-the-horse-into-the-ground measure, not a question of time. But the audience wanted the events to end before the evening's entertainment, and the saddling and waiting and riding made everything late.

The bronc was snubbed to a second horse, a tether while the contestant fought to mount.

They blindfolded the horse, pulled the blindfold off when the rider was seated. That's a blind date.

The contestant rode until the horse tired, shuddered to a stop.

These are the moves:
crowhop and side-step
jackknife and sunfish
sidewind and swap ends
zig-zag and pitch
jolt and twist
jar and plunge

Duck and dodge, spin and buck, twist and snap.

Dancing the outlaw: a bucking horse has mastered the art of climbing ladders made of air.

Blister was one of the best buckers in the world.
Arsenic got his own leather halter tooled with his name.

Recite the names of the great broncs:
>Cotton Picker
>Calico
>Santa Claus
>Flat Creek
>Lightning
>Wildfire
>Tom Thumb
>Glass Eye
>Sage King
>Snow White
>Nickles and Dimes
>Wild Cherry
>Breakaway
>Gaviota
>Tornado
>Flat Tire
>Raggedy Ann
>Saturn Rocket
>Garden Party
>Zip Code

The poetry of their fury.

I'll draw Flat Tire.

Cast in bronze:
>Mad Money
>Labelled Money
>100 Proof
>John Wayne
>Coconut Roll
>Zorro Bandit
>Gin Neat
>Squaw Patch
>Fox
>Calamity Jane
>Chico
>Red Wing
>Skooks

And Cyclone, the original bronc ridden by the original Canadian champ, Tom Three Persons. So wild he had to be thrown down, held on the ground while Three Persons straddled him. Cyclone had bucked off 127 riders, was known as the unrideable black demon, the Black Terror. Could sunfish and swap ends, rear and tumble.

Hard Times should be the name of a bucking horse, a repeat offender: over and over, busted.

Another name for a bucking horse: Relic.

Who christens these animals, the rough stock and rocking names fulfilling dreams of mastery, conquering luxuriant fierceness?

Their lineage is resistance.

Grated Coconut: his rump hit riders in the back, knocking them forward. He was the son of Coconut Roll and Wyatt Earp, grandson of Rolly Polly and Wild Strawberry.

Cindy Rocket bucked for 20 years.

Guilty Cat, Coyote, Gunsmoke, Bottom Line, Party Guy, and Six Shooter did their time.

The champions:
    Papa Smurf and Grated Coconut
    Lonesome Me and Outlaw
    Dish Rag and High Tower

Gone to the pastures of beyond.

Prairie

Prairie puts up with fences and people like grasshoppers, a plague coming in.

pprraaiirriiee

Sound out the word and make it croon:
> it sounds like homesickness
> it sounds like the wind through a crack in the door
> it sounds like scarcity and migration and train whistles and
> political protest

Don't even mention:
> Rupert's Land
> territorial autonomy
> oil
> beef
> alienation

A featureless steppe sculpted by the scrape of glaciation, undulating vistas interrupted by secret coulees.

Cold winters, hot summers, wet years with widespread flooding, followed by dry years of drought and desiccation.

Ah, the rub of myth, of Palliser and his recoil.

Here is where geography gets tired, puzzled, resorts to trickery and guile.

Here is where *prairie* turns to Stampede for comic relief.

Lust

I kissed a cowboy.

Enough already, I finally kissed a cowboy.

Although it was not part of my plan, I decided it was necessary.

For:
> my education
> research
> my blood pressure
> my late lost aunt who always wanted to marry one
> the hail storm that we both survived
> the taste of smoke
> the pile of ribs we didn't eat
> the purebred undershirt

A little late, but better late than never. At my age, one can't be too careless.

No cowboys in my history, although history jostles with cowboys, serious and influential, vaquero grit combined with handshake leverage, a straightforward probity the soul of Stampede. Whatever is western, they are; whatever is frontier, they are; whatever is gumption, they are.

Bareback and tie-down, saddlebronc and bull-rider. Reductive, those labels, buckles on a Sunday belt. Technical skill and timing, strength, coordination and balance. Impossible combinations, preposterous fusion.

Cowboys concretize the dynamic centre of rodeo. They out-spin the midway; surfeit every hamburger and hotdog; resist the huckster purveyors of eatables and drinkables and wearables; outshine the hottest mid-day sun.

But quietly, quiet as dust at midnight, soundless as hush. Bashful, diffident and obliging. No stretch limos, no brass fanfare, no ballyhoo. Just a clip-clop hopalong: you fellows ready to show them how to do this job? Let's move and drop, skate across this dusty dust, skid in the gumbo of rainstorm mud.

They're wearing helmets now, a thin shell of protection between thinking and the hard-packed infield. They don't need to prove they're not romantics but pragmatists, a necessary combination of requirement and extremity.

With a soupçon of dexterity.

The pick-up man is a better bet than the bronc rider – fewer injuries result.

We've picked their pockets, stolen their idiom.

"Cowboy up," we exclaim gleefully, without a hot damn clue what that means or how to pull that "up" off. Cowboy up and don't show the pain, the impossible pain that rides the periphery of the joints having taken their jolting and jolted for good. Susceptible to injury.

"In cahoots," we whisper, conspiratorially.

"He's a bad hoss," we claim, experts on nothing.

We're once-a-year dress-ups, mail-order imitators, with too much mustard on our buns.

They are marked for degree of difficulty, cowboys. At least when they ride, and even more often when they walk or drink or sleep, when they hunker down and rest a moment. They are tired of the myth, the feral gaze that lingers on their legend.

On the road, sleeping in the truck, keeled over an endless cup of coffee, medicine in a tin, liniment, tape yourself and cowboy up or take a leave, back out.

The announcer declares the outcome between horse and bucked-off rider. He used to bray BUCKED OFF. Now he wields a more subdued No Time, summary for biting the dust or getting thrown.

"Help him. Give him a big hand! Long live cowboys."

"Yup," says the clown, safely out of the infield. "Toughen up you wusses."

His form of praise: "He's got a lot of try in him."

Rough stock and pitch, spur and pray.

No wonder I wanted to kiss a cowboy.

I was impressed with his bristle, nine days strong and fierce as the bull he rode. Not to a standstill, but for an eternity, eight seconds stretched out in a thin, attenuated line of balance and foolhardiness, talent and luck.

He hailed from the east, he said, the only personal fact he let slip. A Maritimer and with no experience of the cowboy genre, or so he claimed.

Although he embodied the form well, the squared shoulders, the camouflaging hat, the rolling walk. He fit in with his school, his history of risk and ride, an obdurate connection with saddles.

A fine disguise for a man from High River.

We are the watchers, sideline excursionists, voyeurs and cowards. The Merlot drinkers who know nothing about suitcase handles, rigging or chute or exposure, who have not a bit of cow sense.

Ranch hand. Cowboy nowhere close to boy, but man, perilous and qualified and fearless as he is fearful.

The work of a cowboy:
> break up and separation
> herding
> de-horning and branding

The work of those who watch the cowboy:
> voyeurism

The work of those who tag along with the cowboy:
> side-kickery

Cowboys uncouth and riotous, gentle exuberance playing with peril.

The age of the cowboy.
The spirit of the cowboy.

And me, I was following the cowgirl code:
> get up
> dress up
> show up
> never give up

As for the kissing: he pretended to be reluctant and I pretended to be eager. It was pure détente, an outbreak of Stampede thaw.

Kiss that damn cowboy and get it over with.

Bankrupt

Ranching a tale of economics (just follow the jobs) and transportation (horses again).

Work and horses tied to movement:
> move the cattle
> move the horses
> move the trails
> move the men
> move the cold
> move that hayfield and move those lines west
> move it before the survey parcels it all into pieces

Necessities:
> barbed wire fencing
> campfire lies
> hay bale philosophy

This passing west, lamented or not, time accelerated, flashing in front of the era's own eyes.

Roping and riding's expected, but shooting has been sidelined, left to those who need to hold the soother of a gun, those who rely on number 11 lines between the eyebrows, the tough look of squinting into focus.

And as for frontier, has it disappeared? Did it even exist? Buried somewhere deep inside the memory of July in January.

The vanishing west, the vanishing world, vanishing horses, vanishing sky, vanishing vanishment, the vanishing horizon, the vanishing dream, all vanished. (Held over in the western.)

Ingredients:
> take one lone prairie
> some docile horses
> a few lanky men
> a sky full of nothing

The edge of the city, the edge of the sky, the edge of the edge, and nothing to hold onto.

"Emporium of the vanished world" setting out its wares to tempt disappearance.

Down for the count

Bandwagon and garbage, the stink of fading cordite.

How many hours of rehearsal?

How many chaperones?

How many performers?

Stop counting. Horses and bulls, people and exhibits, coaches and sound checks, clowns and announcers, arenas and dirt, directors and boxes, uniforms and hangnails.

Three hundred pairs of boots bought every day.
At least 300 remedies for blisters.
At least 600 new blisters.

Two million mini-donuts. Millions of visitors, winnings, stuffed animals, exaggerations.

Five tons of baked beans.

Three hundred toilets.

Twenty-two hundred volunteers.

A thousand horses.

Who's counting?

Aftermath

After:
    after the thunderstorms that rolled in herds overhead
    after the hail that pulverized the garden
    after the hangover that followed the hangover that followed
    the hangover
    after the blisters' slow healing
    after the horse trailers have driven away, followed by plumes of dust
    after the last barbecue, the condiments congealing in their bottles
    after the bleachers are cleaned with high-power washers
    after the dirt on the infield is sifted, turned, packed down to wait
    for winter

After all, with nothing left but bad puns, the buck stops here.

Time to salvage hectic insomnia, when the Ctrain runs all night and the
fireworks pop endlessly.

And no, this isn't your first rodeo, not by a country mile.

Get off your high horse, it's time to touch ground, back to work, keep
regular hours and line up appointments, visit the dentist and clean out the
garage, pay the insurance, and buy the kids' school supplies.

Head for the aftermath: divorce lawyers rubbing their hands, STD clinics
jammed, animal rights fundraisers spiking, burst blisters, hangover to the
one hundredth magnitude, sore backs, bankruptcy, overworked ambulance
and rescue services.

Back to work, blinded by the blind-side, the unexpected expropriation, the
market muddle, that terrible wonderful feeling of having been taken out of
your skin, carried to another level of elation and mourning.

Fence/lines reprise

Fences remind fields of confinement and exclusion, escaped boundaries.

Fences separate space from space, air from air.

A fence demonstrates an antelope's jump, betrays a horse's nicker.

Economies again.

First they drew invisible lines, far as the eye could see, the holding defined by a trail, an outcrop, a coyote's den. Grasslands patrolled by line riders who imagined a mark running from that coulee to that creek cut. Riders kept cattle within corrals surrounded by the taste of air. They ride fence still, with post-hole diggers and wire stretchers.

Declare a ranch, grazable land, good grass.

Pay attention to freedom; free range is never free.

Here is the challenge: how do you make a fence stand up in a world where the wind can crush a granary?

The fence was a social revolution, a statement of human ownership. Choose land, build shelter, draw lines across space.

Fences are persuasive, full of guile. Mute eloquence speeching to the grass, a wire on which the wind can bow a violin.

Fences look to distance and its beckon, distinguish one green quilt of field from another. Sheer beauty their stitch and staple, their clothesline suggestion, pointing toward afar.

Elbows akimbo, barbed wire will bite, stickle and stab, a turf war.

Devil's rope, pulling a line from sky to edge. Take care to sit carefully. Come to the point. Catch the shirt-back with a barb.

Barbed wire proposes definite discomfort, speaks with sharp teeth. One strand, electrified, will electrify. Three strands will stretch so tightly that you can write prairie on the spaces between the lines. Or catch the unison of one child holding two strands apart while the other crawls through the gap.

Never put a roll of barbed wire in the living room.

The sky here is a field bigger than it ever needs to be. The fence is its edge, worn on the sleeve of the slow hills:

    and the ranch begat the fence
    and the fence begat the past
    and the past begat the fearful disappearance of history
    and that ghosting begat the Stampede

The tribute to the past, demise staged as a recurrence, its epic remembering determination that the great era of cattle ranching would not disappear into a vague emanation of smoke and dust.

Barbed wire fencing air. The idea of enclosure, measurement, division, grid. A claim arguing property.

The barbed wire design that ultimately won out was Joseph Glidden's, sharp metal barbs twisted around a strand of smooth wire, with a second intertwined piece of wire so the barbs couldn't slide around.

Stole his wife's hairpins to fashion into spikes.

Then took the handcrank coffee grinder off the wall, used the mill to coil the barbs.

Made him a rich man.

Made his wife mad.

Weadick

He first came to Alberta to buy horses. Looked around, liked what he saw. Filed it away as a place to revisit.

1906, one of the famous winters, killed cows by thousands. Those cattle, scabby and long of horn, weren't as tough as they pretended to be and the snow and cold – thermometers at 60 below – froze them in their tracks.

When spring came, rotting carcasses ranked the air; you could smell decaying ranching dreams, the Big Stink, as if to say, "ha, fooled you, and don't you forget it." Gave everybody a case of discouraged.

Weadick returned in 1908 under the moniker Cheyenne Bill, one of the trick ropers in the Miller Brothers' 101 Ranch "Real Wild West Show."

There were plenty of counterfeit wild west shows, disputable and fraudulent, pretending to be authentic. Plenty of circus tricks and bluffers. And what does authenticity measure except its own imitation? The vanishing west, gone to fence, memorialized.

Ranching looked to be going extinct. Gave Weadick the idea for a celebration of that "dying race – the cowboy." Always good to consecrate lost ground, and Weadick took to the idea of memorializing the cowboy romance with a canny vengeance, to "recreate an atmosphere of the frontier days as they really were, devoid of far-fetched fiction." A likely story.

Guy Weadick wrote letters until his hand was sore. Hard to imagine a man with spurs like his and a sore hand. He wrote to prime ministers and dukes, to cowboys and stock breeders, persuaded them the Stampede was worth the trip. People who came: Peter B. Kyne, Frazier Hunt, Tom Mix, Hoot Gibson, Earl Haig. And more.

Weadick kept in touch. Wrote to Will James: "when I go up again, I'm thinking of making a noise on your back porch." Was that a promise or a threat?

He talked until his hand was aching, claimed extravagant metaphors. "I would say to you, that we are going to have the buckinest bucking horses that ever bucked a buck."

He was relentless, clamoring that it would be a regular "Hum Dinger." Sales pitch the world, a "monster celebration." Wanted to throw a big party, succeeded. Threw a few more. And then a few more. Loved the party and the whiskey.

And determined that the Stampede would be all-inclusive, hastening "to assure everyone, no matter where they come from what their nationality is, nor what their color may be, a square deal. What they have to do to get the money is to show they are the best first second and third in the events in which they have entered in."

He wasn't the most grammatical man, and punctuationally challenged, but he was persuasive, could talk up his gathering with the best of hucksters.

He travelled with a typewriter and hammered out his pleas and persuasions with equal force. Where is that typewriter now? Gone to grass.

His favourite horse was called Snip.

He got letters from the likes of R.B. Bennett commenting on his untiring efforts. The Governor General sent "best thanks for your invitation to partake of a cowboy breakfast on September 6th."

The "Department of Indian Affairs," those federal bureaucrats, writing from Winnipeg, wanted strict guidelines. "As you know, there are many abuses accruing to the Red man when brought in contact with a certain class of whites, and to obviate these, the Fair and City authorities must be prepared to co-operate with the Department." They must delineate "camps which can be easily policed and patrolled … transportation and rationing arranged and a schedule made of when and where they are wanted for parades, etc."

The government's favourite ploy: paperwork.

The Indian Agent wrote to Weadick about Tom Three Persons, who "has made up his mind to enter and he wants to enter for the two bucking contests."

And he did. And he won. The only Canadian to take one of the named competitions.

But the real winner was Weadick.

"An International Event of Distinction held in its Natural Environment, Devoid of Sham, Rehearsal, Exaggeration or Affectation." Was he drunk or intoxicated?

He was not sober.

A cowpuncher in his younger days, now the impresario looking for a place to plant his idea, scouring the west for opportunity. Found it here.

His legs were so long he needed tall horses.

Narrow as a quirt.

Some say he was an unrepentant hedonist, and he had the looks, bedroom eyes and a sulky mouth.

He was a man who was hard to manage, but nothing in Stampede is easily scripted. These raw contests lacked gentility. We come by the heritage honestly.

Later in life he tried to become a writer. His manuscript of miscellaneous tales about cowboys and the cowboy life was rejected. The letters from Lorne Pierce at Ryerson Press are cold and academic. Rejected.

He might not have been much of a writer, but he was one damn fine talker.

1912 Orders

A parade every day – at 9:00 a.m.

Roping and Ropers
Broncho Riding
Cowgirls' Broncho Riding
Cowboys' Relay Race
Ladies' Relay Race
Indian Relay Race
Bareback Riding
Wild Horse Race
Steer Bulldogging
Trick Riding by Cowboys
Fancy Riding by Cowgirls
Stage Coach Race

Good Horses and Good Clothes go Hand in Hand

Whoop-La!!!

Welcome Cowboys! This City is Yours!

DO YOU THINK "the Stampede" Would Make a Good Annual Event?
If so, advise us. This is Some Country, and all are Welcome.
If you Like our Show, tell your Friends. If you don't, – tell us.
ADIOS.

~ FRONTIER DAYS COMMITTEE, PER GUY WEADICK, MGR

Turning tricks

Weadick met Flores in Chicago, and married her in 1905, in Memphis, Tennessee.

He didn't need to write letters to Flores, they were the *"premiers maîtres du lasso americain."*

He knew he was second fiddle to Prince, her trained horse.

Untrained he was, but pliable. Became part of the team that became a trick performance.

What she could do:
  Original upside down spinning on horseback
  Spinning 22 feet of rope on running horse
  Straight catch on horse back – horse's head
  Spinning catch on horse back – horse's feet
  Straight catch – horse and rider
  Turn over catch – horse's feet
  Over hand catch – rider
  Front spin – horse's feet
  Back spin – horse's feet
  Jumping through rope once – horse's feet
  Jumping through rope twice – horse's feet
  Kicking rope with foot – horse's feet
  Back butterfly – horse's head
  Bounding rope – horse's feet
  Spinning loop around body – horse's feet
  Tail catch – horse's tail
  Routine of butterfly spinning
  Reversing rope three ways (Ocean wave)
  Knot tying – two hard knots – one single bow
  Skipping rope
  Half hitching – two ways
  Routine of flat spinning and rope dance
  Spinning 65 feet of rope on running horse

Now that's one hell of a repertoire. She didn't bother roping him.

He was a lean liar, a long drink of water. Gaunt even, his bones resembling the frame of a horse.

He combined that wide-brimmed hat with a bandana and a businesslike set of gauntlets, and if anyone commented on the bowtie, he looked petulant and embarrassed. He got more handsome as he grew older, lost his American look, although the drink took its toll. That was back when men were sunburned and hard-handed.

Lived at the Stampede Ranch, High River, from 1920 to 1947.

He was always the tallest man in the photographs, half a head above the others. Wide eyes and an innocent face made him more persuasive.

Dolly Mullens, a figure in the shadows, married Weadick after Flores died. There has to be a story there, a sleight of hand. Difficult to cut that knot.

In the archives a cursive note from Dolly, dated May 11, 1953. She gives him a scolding, tells him, "I am very sick and tired of putting up with and is one of the reasons which I have definitely decided to dissolve this unpleasant partnership and there is nothing you can say or do which will make me change my mind. I want to forget the whole affair … . Please don't make yourself a nuisance by knocking on my door at all hours of the night."

She wasn't much for grammar or punctuation either. But her sentiments were clear.

From Vaudeville to High River to Phoenix. From Flores LaDue to pissed-off Dolly. The cycles of what can't cure you can kill you. And not softly.

Because he wanted to throw a big party, he held the first Stampede in the fall, when he hoped farmers had finished the harvesting. He was nostalgic for the past, its vanishing ways, became a promoter of participatory memory.

Weadick died in Los Angeles in 1953, a mere 68, and not even old. He must have been disappointed when he looked out of the window. That ache in his hat. From Alberta to L.A.

Buried in High River, next to Flores.

Horse litigation

Weadick was fair and unfair. A hard man to argue with.

Wanted the best that money couldn't buy. The suppliers of bucking horses balked, gave him Midnight, branded with a door key on the left thigh. And Ray "just got sulky and did not go very good because he was mad and did not have enough room, he always wanted lots of air."

So did Weadick.

Word got around. "They are sure very particular in what they take, the slightest blemish or over seven years or less than 15 hands turns a horse down." Cannon Ball, Red Pepper, and Chain Lightning, all injured. The owner wanted compensation for Chain Lightning.

And then there were those pesky out-of-pocket expenses, the way the Stampede eats money.

Gentleman outlaw Geo Francis wrote to "friend Guy" from Hotel Havre, Montana, on December 17, 1919:

> "As for myself, I am getting along nicely, just passing the time away in town this winter, loving my friends and fighting my enemies. I have beaten them twice in the supreme court since I saw you. I guess they think I am a hard old cat to frame up on.
>
> "We are getting a real old time cow killer of a winter here. Cattle and horses are dying by the thousands, and if it continues much longer most of my enemies will be herding sheep or working on the section in the spring."
>
> ~ Geo S. Francis

Treaty Seven

This gathering place for thousands of years, the confluence of the Bow and the Elbow, the mergence of two streams a perfect spot.

The federal Indian agents tried to keep the First People away, but Weadick argued and pulled strings and swore. They were still restricted, but came anyway, provided the "Indian" for the stampede equation.

Reverend John McDougall took home $390 for furnishing Indians. And what did they take home?

The participation of First Nations people: celebration or exploitation?

2000 of the people dignified that first parade.

And who translated for Weadick? Calf Robe, that venerable name, now a bridge famous for its treacherous icing and always mispronounced by Calgarians. Think a Robe is a Rope. Nope.

View

The view from under a hat, a shading hand, the kaleidoscope faces.

Cowboy hats used to be bigger, tougher, meant for work more than decoration.

The photographer's view, the slit under the grandstand, the feet of the horses.

The view from between a horse's ears, perked.

The view from the infield, the thunder underfoot.

The view from under his belt.

Is it the view to the west, the mountains? Some vista that persuades us to undertake the irrational?

Here on the divide, between the foothills and the plains.

Everyone's got an opinion.

Robert Bott in *The New York Times,* May 29, 1983:
> "For 355 days of the year, sophisticated Calgarians try to
> forget that this was once a cowtown – and that it may be one
> again after the petroleum peters out. But for 10 days in July,
> everyone digs up a Stetson and dons pointy boots to play
> cowboy. Founded in 1912 and running from July 8 to 17 this
> year, the Stampede is not just a Brobdingnagian country fair,
> it is also a municipal catharsis, a country-western equivalent
> to Mardi Gras."

Who thinks this sarcasm is funny?

Depends on the point of view.

Vintage

Watchword for the past.

And what does Stampede have to do with grapes and their fermentation? Is this the same as retro? A vogue period?

Romance the cowboy, nostalgia the old west that wasn't ever old, and didn't have a chance to get middle-aged. A sepia scrim, that calming amber shade overcasting long years of repetition.

Echo that queasy era of sputters and false starts:
>1912, and the first Stampede, a test run, hailed as a success and then suspended;
>1919, the Victory Stampede, homage to returning cowboys and soldiers.

1923, the real beginning. No Mulligan this time, combined with the Exhibition, chuckwagon racing introduced, finally earned a profit, has continued since.

Is our vintage abject or brash, obsolete despite its yearly reprise?

Or the best of its kind:
>vintage western
>vintage hallucination
>vintage for the nonce and nothing else
>a chance to cram a hat on, and pretend that yesterday is tomorrow

Ripe or classical, but never venerable, this mad celebration of dust and debris.

Stampede. There is only one, and that is Calgary's.

Watch your language

When did the word "Stampede" appear in popular discourse? Weadick considered it his word, his property, even tried to trademark it, made it part of his lawsuit.

Litigious: should be the name of another bucking horse.

Weadick knew its origins well enough: American/Mexican Spanish *estampida,* from the Spanish, crash, from *estampar* to stamp.

This sudden rush and flight, a word for two hundred years.

Stampede.

1835: Washington Irving in *A Tour on the Prairies.* He wanted to sketch the plains, explore the Far West. After 17 years "abroad," he needed inspiration, returned to America and in September of 1832 went on his western tour with some companions, eager to experience the wild west. It wasn't so wild or so west, but he got to Oklahoma and the Red River of the south. The man we think of as a consummate New Yorker didn't get very far, but he wielded the term we have come to apply to people and animals, somewhere by the north fork of the Red River, a scamper of horses in the night.

"We encamped, towards evening, in a valley, beside a scanty pool, under a scattered grove of elms, the upper branches of which were fringed with tufts of the mystic mistletoe. In the course of the night the wild colt whinnied repeatedly; and about two hours before day there was a stampedo, or sudden rush of horses, along the purlieus of the camp, with a snorting, and neighing, and a clattering of hoofs, that startled most of the rangers from their sleep, who listened in silence until the sound died away, like the rushing of a blast. As usual, the noise was at first attributed to some party of marauding Indians; but, as the day dawned, a couple of wild horses were seen in a neighbouring meadow, which scoured off on being approached. It was now supposed that a gang of them had dashed through our camp in the night. A general mustering of our horses took place; many were found scattered to a considerable distance, and several were not to be found. The prints of their hoofs, however, appeared deeply dinted in the soil, leading off, at full speed, into the waste; and their owners, putting themselves on the trail, set off in weary search of them."

1874: Mountie Sam Steele experienced a similar occasion at Fort Dufferin, just before the outset of the trek west:

> "A thunderbolt fell in the midst of the horses. Terrified, they broke their fastening and made for the corral. The six men on guard were trampled underfoot as they tried to stop them. The maddened beasts overturned the huge wagons, dashed through a row of tents, scattered everything, and made for the gate of the large field in which we were encamped. In their mad efforts to pass they climbed over one another to the height of many feet … . Crazed with fright, the horses crossed the river and continued their flight on the opposite bank, and the majority were between 30 and 50 miles in Dakota before they were compelled by sheer exhaustion to halt.
>
> "I shall never forget that night. I had full view of the stampede, being not more than 50 yards from the horses as they rushed at the gate and attempted to pass it, scrambling and rolling over one another in one huge mass. This and the unceasing flashes of lightning, the rolling of the thunder, the loud shouts of the troopers as they vainly attempted to stop the horses and the mad gallop of Colman's team, gave to it a weird and romantic complexion, typically suggestive of the wild west."

"Suggestive of the wild west," a wild they wanted, did all they could to build that story.

Started Stampede:
    first livestock hub of Alberta
    beef and more beef
    bulls and horses
    sheep and their sheepishness
    dogs and ponies in their traces
    swine proliferated
    not to mention goats and llamas
    ostriches and workhorses and morgans
    sixteen classes of Holstein dairy cattle.
    a dozen poultry varieties and now just plastic chickens

Herd

We raised cattle on our farm, slow fat steers and slippery calves that dotted the pasture. No riding those steers, no roping them either. We corralled them gently, food and not entertainment.

Leasehold rules long gone. Grazing a lost verb.

100,000 acres for a penny an acre a year. One cow for every ten acres. What kind of math is that? What kind of bargain with space is that?

Calgary:
> this little settlement huddled under the high hills around, crouched by the river, in disbelief at the sheer intensity of light

> this ramshackle collection of shacks, temporary as their occupants, lean-to as their ambition

Ranching and farming:
> another version of gambling

Sales:
> we'll sell you a cowboy hat
> a pair of spurs
> a square foot of hot air

Mud and blood together:
> the green kids from farms out on the prairie, eager for sport, get a whiff of the corral and the race, just a bit of animal, that mad dash

What's gone:
> Wild cow milking
> Wild horse racing
> Quarter horse racing
> Bull-dogging

Stampede tamed down to a less-than-thoroughly-western event. And what is western anyway? Background to a movie, a case of indigestion, a vaudeville rip-off?

What's your bar tab?

Don't critique your whooping it up:
    call it a western rush, not a gold rush
    ride that scooter over the grounds
    pull the beer lever

In 1966 the first colour television showed a film of rodeo horses being driven to the Calgary Stampede.

Rope-spinning monologists with experience in Buffalo Bill Cody's Wild West show told tall tales.

The 1942 movie *Calgary Stampede,* renamed "Riding High," was revised to an American rather than Canadian background, with Victor Moore, Dick Powell, Mary Martin, and Marjorie Reynolds.

Senator Pat Burns' giant birthday cake at the Stampede in 1931 was cut into 25,000 pieces and distributed to everyone.

Fragments and pieces, herded together.

From a distance

Calgary pretends to be cow town. Big business, faux straw bales, glass teepees.

And is it true that the rugged folk of western Canada come together in Calgary or is this now a space for the less rugged to pretend, pull on a pair of expensive boots and strut?

Is this our natural setting, the pathways beside the Bow with their sprinkling of sodbusters, oilmen and ranch hands?

Next stop, next stop, next stop, a pit stop enroute to the Rockies.

Let the world gas about how sophisticated we aren't, liking the taste of dust, the rowdy of rowdy.

This semi-arid plain, sere with all that will vanish, a vanishing world memorialized here.

Grace notes

Wilf Carter:
>from a Nova Scotian lumberjack to a cowboy in the Blue Canadian
>Rockies
>performed at the Stampede in 1964

Ian Tyson:
>came back west from Toronto, and never left again
>Parade Marshall in 2012

Corb Lund:
>fever and pain
>forgiveness and hurt

Bull

These are the bulls that rock the cowboys to sleep:
Lowlife
Smoke Show
Bottle Rocket
Grand Slam
Heavens Basement

Outlaw, 1000 kg of muscle and mad. Seventy-one jumps out of the chute, and ridden only once. Lived to old age and was buried at the Stampede Ranch.

It is the height of the rodeo.

"Are you ready for some bull riding?"

Terror and bloodlust and adrenalin.

These are the offspring of the winged bulls of Nineveh, a human head merged with a bull's body, the horns and ears of a bull, and wings, intricate feathers that lift the stone into life.

The ancient Assyrians knew the coiled force of the bull's body waiting to spring, its dangerous politics. Their taut, muscular legs and impassive human faces declared their danger. Sennacherib, who laid out that city and its unrivalled palace, who commissioned those great stone beasts, set them to guard Nineveh's 15 gates, then tempered them with the ranch of hanging gardens, near the river Tigris. The garden in the desert, the hanging green defying the desert with its feats of irrigation, all an early forecast for this Calgary. Sennacherib would have valued the Stampede, its buzzing intensity.

These are the *lamassu* come to life, rancid and evocative. It is the power of the hybrid, half bull, half human, that makes our blood leap, the impassive face of the man atop the bull, one hand aloft, that returns us to the awe of that celestial reference, the man riding what symbolized a household protective spirit, guardians of the doors that lead to the heart of a city.

Nineveh, that Babylon, the city of Gilgamesh, his epic dream of battling wild bulls.

Cowboys I have known

Their arena was the thrashed and cactus-rich circle of dirt down beside the Battle River.

They were boys practising, riding the steers they could manage to catch, cooling their bruises in the muddy river.

They wanted to be cowboys, worked their way hand over hand on the ropes, getting splinters from rail fences.

They never made the big time, the Stampede's culling of the best of the best of the best, were never invited to compete. No, these were boys at country rodeos, eager for the distant glamour of buckles and bruises.

They weren't the kind to turn into husbands.

Surprise

Ladies and gentlemen, step right up and prepare to see the unexpected:
>see the dirigible burn
>see horses jumping over cars
>see cowboys die
>see an aviatrix dancing on the wings of a plane
>see Fred McCall land his biplane on the needle of the merry-go-round
>>(not crash but accident, two kids in the passenger seat, who probably turned off the ignition. McCall had no choice but to set down on the pole. Miraculously, no one was hurt. But it started a Stampede, people racing to cut a piece of canvas from the plane as a memento.)
>see the Victory Stampede of 1919, celebrating the end of the war
>see the grandstand as ski-jump
>>(1921, a 75-foot steel tower and ski-jump were built on top of the grandstand.)
>see a bleak Calgary winter selling snow
>see the outriders turning the barrels
>see the last remaining liars tell the truth

Big crowds are expected.

What is the attraction?

Nostalgia for the past, the holster and the guns?

Mourning the recent past?

Claiming the future?

Midway

Its raucous price, the slide show of sleight of hand and its undoing.

Dancing girls, three-legged calves, an opera cloak made of prairie chicken feathers, clairvoyants side by side with ice-wagons, palmistry, acrobats, and ferris wheels, gambling and horse races.

Pinkertons to foil the pickpockets and confidence men.

Now tamed to a few games of ringette, over-priced slices of pizza, the spun fakery of candy floss beside a carny running a wheel and apples dipped in bacon fat.

A magnet for:
    short-change artists
    vagrants
    pickpockets
    prostitutes
    crooks and crooners
    drunks and drinkers

All side by side.

Somebody had to say it: "The unquestionably immoral effect of the midway should commend itself to our social reform leagues."

Now and then.

Do your goddamn homework

I take visitors to the Stampede:
>an academic who teaches at the Sorbonne
a computer tech who lives in Stuttgart
a sewing instructor from Oviedo
a skier from Innsbruck
a dairy farmer from Australia
a writer from Delhi
my friends from Vancouver and Winnipeg

I refuse to host journalists because they won't do their homework, think that Nashville North and the music stage and the midway are the main story. Don't understand why shorts and a t-shirt aren't allowed in the infield. Don't recognize the privilege of seeing a cowboy's hands bleeding. They think it's an act, a trick.

Or the university professor who said, after watching the Chucks, "I don't get it. Just a bunch of horses and wagons in a messy swirl down in the ring."

Do your goddamn homework. Do some research.

Pay attention to what's going on, the contest between human and animal. Animals always win. The humans splinter and bleed.

Don't expect rodeo to be a sweet sport, bloodless and sanitized.

The romance of trick riders, steer wrestlers and cowboys unrealistic. Born out of blood.

Like bulldogging, now outlawed: that leap from the saddle of a galloping horse to the back of a full-grown steer, the cowboy grabbing its horns, twisting to reach the steer's upper lip, biting the steer's lip, then releasing the horns, raising his arms and twisting the animal to the ground with his mouth. Tore their horns out by the roots, the spurting blood a sign of machismo. Who invented this sport, this mad kiss?

I take a Swedish masseuse to the Ranchman's, the floor cleared for line dancing, the shooter girl ready with her *cowboy cocksuckers,* butterscotch schnapps and Irish cream and goldschlager. Set you right back on your ass if you have more than one. Two-step till you're sore.

Or the *pickled cowboy*, tequila and lime juice and pickled bean juice. Or the *cowboy's breakfast*, bourbon and maple syrup with candied bacon as a garnish.

Just bring me a Stampede Caesar, made with bourbon and steak sauce. Add a lot of garnish, beans and celery. Yep, I wanted a salad.

Slip the traces of this cowboy story, turn around and look over your shoulder, the sadness that follows the day after Stampede is over, another year gone, another summer almost turning to dusk.

Where is here?

Behind the sunglasses lurk the eyes, steady or blinking,

The arms crossed across the chest, faces tight-lipped as they wait for a verdict.

It's the way my butt looks in jeans, solid and uncompromised, like I've been holding down a chair for a good few years.

Everybody's hair looks better under a hat, until the hat comes off and the face goes naked again.

There is a way to lean against a fence, a contemplative stance that suggests experience, the distance gaze, the what-are-we-waiting-for tilt.

The patience of buffalo and the wiliness of coyotes.

Where are the coyotes in Stampede lore? They lurk along the edges of the city's ravines, observe from the cover of bushes. They are there, on the fringes of the grounds, a shadow crossing the unwinding past.

Apology

Preserve the west. Stew it and can it and bottle it. Line it up on a shelf in the cold room, preserves shining with industry and frugality.

Demonstrate. Not the demonstrate we know now, but the old-fashioned kind of demonstrate, a show, an explanation, an educational performance that explains and explicates.

Stampede becomes catachresis, a mis-application, that desire to turn watching into a version of participatory demonstration. To be the object of a demonstration is to watch and to learn. The Stampede teaches danger and delight in strange potions.

Triumphalism: okay, beat the stuffing out of me, it's a triumphalist story, with winners and losers against that mural of a big sky.

Don't try to trick me; this isn't my first rodeo.

The city loves Stampede, embraces it, enjoys it.
Reviles it, excoriates it, repudiates it.

What's the myth? It could be a curse word, mythology and its misdirection, all about the heart instead of the head. Disappointment and debt, the pull of a dream deferred. Why not settle for a rodeo?

The myths of Stampede:
   real action
   real cowboys
   real horses
   roping, riding, rooting

More than a backdrop, a practised set of performers?

Victoria Park

She was gone already, the beady-eyed queen. The neighbourhood named after her, she still on the throne in 1900, but gone by 1912 when the first Stampede erupted.

Still there, Victoria Park, beltline and cycle track, warehouses and funeral homes.

Alberta named for Princess Caroline Louise Alberta, fourth daughter of Queen Victoria.

Alberta labelled in honour of her father, the dead Prince Albert.

Married to John Campbell, Marquess of Lorne, who declared, bored to death out in the staid and decorous east, "If I were not GG of Canada, I would be a cattle rancher in Alberta."

He was not quite out of the closet but loved travelling for its freedoms, loved camping out with the cowboys. Came west and named this district after his wife, unhappy fourth daughter, as all fourth daughters are.

The princess never made it here, bypassed Alberta by taking the train through the United States to San Francisco and then up to Victoria. Used the rigours of a Canadian winter as an excuse for everything.

And did she try to prevent the Marquess's night prowls by bricking up the windows?

He wanted to be a cattle rancher, suspicious of bathing, ready to subscribe to second sight, and protective of his billiard table – out of bounds for the ladies.

That was a marriage enabled by distance. Absence makes the heart placated.

The ranch

We yearn to recapture what we have never seen but dreamed.

It must be out there somewhere:
> the blue hills drenched in audible quiet
> the knuckles of the rail fence grazing beside the dirt track
> the poem of a road with a spine of grass up the middle
> that country road that has seen neither gravel nor bitumen
> only the clop of hooves, the scuff of feet

Covet a working ranch on the Highwood, the smell of sage and insolvency.

Ranches are having a grass holiday.

Now that is an understatement.

Ranches broken up into wheat fields.

Not a word about cool season fescue, or tallgrass prairie to the east. It's shortgrass here, that loll and roll of tough stalks pretending to be endless, deep deep roots centuries old tapping mere traces of water, dense nutrition in their long memories.

The grass that covered this country. Cool season grass, slow-growing, drought-resistant.

Giving the lie to Calgary's irrigation heat, no hesitation, prone to drought and deluge, one after the other.

Semi-arid and the Stampede as wet as any event can be, a wet bar on the move looking for some grass to mow.

The benediction of the gods: good grass.

"Grasses belong to the large family *Gramineae* (or *Poaceae;* the grass family), and form the dominant vegetation of many areas of the world. The possession of a growing point that is mainly at ground level makes grasses suitable as the food of many grazing animals, and for use in lawns and playing fields."

Love

Let me demonstrate a Lazy S.

It sleeps on its back.

My favourite horse breaker was Harry Longabaugh. He did not use an alias in Alberta, but went by his real name, Henry Longabaugh. He was quiet and good with horses. No mention of his abilities with women or his future as a bank robber. No hint that he would become his own mythology, the Sundance Kid.

He worked at the Bar U, hiding out from his early indiscretions, listed in the Canadian census of 1891 as a horse breaker. Could read and write, had a pleasant face, well-liked by all.

He was the American lover we all look for. The cowboy from across the line. A visit and then vamoose. A trace and then gone.

Money

Open the west to cattle ranching and to homesteading. The legendary leasehold offer of 100,000 acres for a penny an acre a year.

A penny an acre a year, inconceivable now, when the penny has vanished and the acre transformed to hectare, when a year is a series of compressed seconds that fly past the idea of time.

The origins of this story lend to an act of persuasion.

Alexander Mackinnon Burgess. Deputy minister, Department of the Interior, 1884. Couldn't ride very well. Bucked off. Broke his collarbone, one of the most commonly broken bones in the human body. Bivouaced with Colonel James Walker, who alternately nursed him and informed him that he'd break the other clavicle if he didn't sell those 94 acres of crown land tucked into the curve of the Elbow River.

The Dominion of Canada grumpily acceded, $2.50 an acre, demanded $235 to be paid immediately. Mortgage foreclosed in 1899. R.B. Bennett acquired the land as speculative property (Prime Ministers broker strange deals). Sold it back to the city of Calgary and the city of Calgary bought that cow pasture in 1901.

Caveat on the title: the land had to be used for an exhibition or it would be reclaimed by Ottawa.

That became the Stampede Grounds.

Take a brewery and a few sandstone buildings, mix them with bragging and exaggeration, load up on optimism, advertise free land, open spaces, a wind so vehement it will tear your ears off. Bring in a passel of land agents and show them Shangri la, become a roundhouse for dissemination. Shout louder than shouting.

That became the seed of Stampede, the shouting and hollering, the elbowing and buttonholing, the crowbarring for donations. Money under the table and over the table, money promised and money pocketed.

Gate receipts and pari-mutuel betting, admission and ratepayers and turning a profit before turning the other cheek.

How much did the pick-up men get paid? $8 a day.

Sneak thieves, pickpockets and hustlers, grifters and drifters.

Gamble:
> win a car
> win a boat
> win a pot of gold
> win a house with a sidewalk attached
> win a horseshoe and hope it brings you luck again.

If you ever had any luck that wasn't bad.

Chance and its chances betray us:
> I put down a marker on the black
> should have bet on red
> fortunate, unfortunate, improbable
> a chance to win real money

Merely a mere shibboleth, this luck and its germinations.

I didn't climb on the horse.
I didn't fall off.

Pure luck.

Handicrafts

Enter:
>pleated aprons
>antimacassars
>stockinettes
>knit and purl
>crocheted pot holders
>lacemaking and fancy work and quilting
>embroidered pillows, collars and cuffs.

Debate the awards given to the best quilts. Sometimes third place is better than first.

Cake decorating:
>extravagant sugar arts
>decorated cakes
>fondant roses
>chocolate foliage
>sponge balls and coconut mountains
>sculptured footballs made of gum paste

Test the shape of pastillage and marzipan, cake mere structural support for the icing.

Show off the age of elegance in western dress, silk blouses and decorated split skirts.

School work:
>music
>art
>penmanship

Horticultural displays:
>warty squash
>bottled carrots
>beet pickles

Cake decorating, multi-layered and terrible-tiered.

Symbolic of labour: it can be certain that the lady from Nightingale who won the blue ribbon does not remember sumptuary laws, the luxury of almonds, ginger, and saffron, or gilded figures made of sugar paste or Henry VIII of England enacting a law specifying the quantity of sugar a cake might have, possibly to control or tax this prevailing convention.

The extravagance of sugar, how in 1527 Cardinal Wolsey served a feast for the French embassy, including miniatures of castles and churches, even the Spire of St Paul's, and figures of beasts and birds and well known personages, only eclipsed by a whole chess set made of sugar paste.

Once sugar was prescribed as a medicine, before it became a luxury before it became a commodity and a commonplace.

Eat

$100 hot dog and cockroach pizza

Deep fried pickles, potato chips on a stick

Cactus burgers

Jurassic pork

Ribs

Corn dogs and candy floss

Nothing containing real vegetables

No vitamins allowed

1923: "The highlight of Saturday night was a buffalo barbeque where over 11,800 barbequed buffalo sandwiches were served up to all paying customers. Five buffalo in total were donated by the federal government, four were cooked at the P. Burns & Co. plant and one was roasted in front of the grandstand."

Eat your words.

Rules

Do not enforce themselves.

Reinvented, changed every year,

Refuse to buck, stroll into the field and sniff for oats.

In the photographs the white blouses shine whiter than white.

Cowboys' faces are darkened by sun and time and cowboy-hood, the tension they win as faux-heroes.

Chiascuro or mendacity, the blood is real, the track is watered, the crowds are illusory as the idea of ranching.

The dust that rose from the infield and the bucking horses settled on the clothes hung on the lines of Mount Royal, leaving a trace that couldn't be easily erased.

These acts outrage finer sensibilities.

Of course we don't have that relationship to animals now.

A finale to the vanishing range.

But not over yet, the nostalgia persists and the smell of competition still surges.

Rules that are not rules, rules that can be changed, rules fluctuating, "the management reserves the right to make any additional rules that circumstances may demand to govern any event."

Rules are meant to be thwarted.

The Board

The mysterious directorate who run the Stampede: used to be range men and cow men and ranchers and stock producers.

Now they're lawyers, accountants and financiers, geologists and architects and dealers in commercial real estate and agri-business and insolvency, steel and oil and gas men, with the occasional barrel racer and fashion mavin for seasoning.

But they carry on, inject some Weadick juice into their veins, and persist, every year another Stampede.

Forgotten the wistful past, the early days of Ernie Richardson, with his baby face and sensual lips, his eyes dreamy behind his spectacles, the force behind the event, the balance to Weadick's bluster, the accountant and the secretary and the bean counter.

Someone's got to be accountable.

Definitions, a coda

How to drink: out of pitcher
Hands: calloused
Floors: sawdust
Legs: jeans
Feet: blistered
Ritual: ten days of sleepless nights
Our adultery: cattle
Nostalgia: isn't what it's cracked up to be, creaking with extinction and forgetfulness
Conception: baby spike nine months later
Western décor: wagon wheels and bales of hay, the opposite of chic

Rodeo: mid-19th-century from Spanish, from *rodear* "go around", based on Latin *rotare,* "rotate".

How to shock a crowd: wear harem pants and pantaloons

How to rope the air: wedding rings, Texas skips, butterflies, ocean waves, and vertical loops

The death trail: doing cowboy tricks in Canada

The day of the cowboy: dead

Ranching: fenced

The wild west: didn't happen here.

There are theories about this: we'll have to do it all over again.

Feeling ourselves at home, we square dance in the cul de sac.

You never know why you love something, but when you do, you cherish its faults as much as its strengths.

Shooting a saskatoon

This west, the story goes, is a real place, with sky and sagebrush, with a smell and a swagger and a whiskey swig sweetness uncorrupted by language. In this real west the distilled perfections of mornings and afternoons and evenings are not just observed or articulated but tasted, touched, worn.

The westness of west. How is it possible to insist on such liturgical companionship, human bondage imposed on a largely indifferent land and space? The west's round-up has ridden the cusp between literal and imaginary, difference and its discontents, the knots of invention and actuality. For all that westerners argue notions of construction and invention, fashion and fusion, spirituality and secularity, gender and ethnicity, the west remains elusive, at cross-purposes with both celebrants and detractors. A monster of indifference and mistress of camouflage, this west performs as escape artist and tightrope walker, ineradicably beautiful, and oh so silently eloquent.

We westerners are in thrall to our own private wests, wests we tame and possess, wests we conquer and abuse, wests we succumb to, swoon before, wests we both worship and pleasure. The west is a virus, a nightclub, a chain letter. The west is a door and a window, neither and both, transparent but private, directive and orientative for all that it is not nor ever will be east. We live in a corner of the universe where the sun sets instead of rising, and yes, going west is a metaphor for death.

Go west, we say: a curse, and a blessing. Die, perish, disappear. And while you're at it, tie yourself up in knots trying to consign the west to oblivion.

The west is a billowing sheet on a clothesline, a correction line, dead reckoning, a sextant. The west is its own best friend, a state of shadow, out of bounds but still a safety zone, beyond the law despite a courthouse full of hanging judges. A crooked compass full of wind and water and lack of both, quick to scold but without bishops or emperors to make decrees, to turn the grasses away from their own bend.

If the west is the best, near or far, lying or truthful, central or peripheral, sinking or rising, bound by nothing more concrete than time's ineffable dimension, then why do we try so hard to pin it down to a minute, or an hour? If a westerner travels west around the world, that westerner will eventually lose a day. Where does the day disappear to?

For all our tough talk about frontiers and duelling doors, their saloon slap, for all our up-to-the-minute arguments about multiples and their heterologies, for all our careful avoidance of sexual innuendoes and old love affairs, the west is where all trails grow faint, where the line between literal and imaginary fades. The west is an elevator big enough to hold a bumper crop, infinitely laconic. Such charisma, such terrible liminality, is past frightening. Somewhere in the myth is a story about cabbages as big as children, about winds so strong they pick up horses, about floods sweeping away whole towns.

But there is a sinister side. West is due and do, past its due date and full of survival's botulism. Who can believe cardinal points and pioneer winds curled up with log cabin quilts made by cowgirls and horseboys, sixguns and silky lariats? Lariat and its largo can never be said the same way twice, threading through the keyhole of the square dance. As for jeans, not to mention boots, charisma and its post-fashionable fashion will outlast a bull-rider any day of the week. Include a grub bag of everything else: ham and legs, buffalo burgers, flapjacks and double axioms, politics and the briberies of prohibition. Marry the dustbowl. And be realistic: for all the shooting that goes on, nobody dares to die in the west. Get a prescription for survival. There's no time for burying or marrying: those passé gestures of permanence have been adamantly and inadequately over-compensated for by time and its foothills environs. Not to mention a few productive oil and gas wells. On the edge out here.

The edge of what?

If only we could knot the west into a handkerchief of distinguishable landforms. But the west won't fit. A westerner can tie that inconvenient body up again and again, even throw it on a few railroad tracks and wait for climactic trains to come along, but there will always be some unidentified limb, some arm or leg sticking out, capable of spontaneous regeneration. We're stuck with the commotion of a naming.

Where does the west begin?
Bad question.
Where will the west end?
Worse question.
Will the west ever end? Unanswerable question.
Is the west sick of its endlessness? Probably.

A derivative of wrestle that won't fit into wrangler, even though it does its best to sneak through the back door of weather's acronym. The west's real adversary is weather, the unexpected cloudburst, the sibulent chinook. That's the best part of west: entice, beguile, cajole. Time to scrub the mud-room floor after a few days of wet weather, and no west is the west if it's raining. Where never is heard a discouraging word, and the skies are not cloudy or grey. A likely story. Of course, it snowed yesterday, or so the weatherman told the sky, and it could go up to 20 tomorrow.

If this is the west, is this the west? Where is the west? Inspissate: thicken by evaporation, something that happens too quickly on the high, dry, parched, hoarse, arid, thirsty plain. Only a drink will evaporate drought and prohibition, no bootleggers in sight.

West of what?

Time to survey the boundaries. Outsiders want the west to lassoo everything into one giant round-up: the laughter and the gunfire and the barbiturate teeth of those inspiring mountains clustered along the horizon's edge. The central view demands that we loop west together with a solipsistic knot that names itself invention. Maybe west's occupants lean toward the literal, but the west is still a knot that no one can cut, Gordian or not, tongue-tied, a double positive. And writhing in the confines of resistance, the west suffers that flay of skin, rope burn that resists any salve or treatment calling itself soothing. Despite every day having to walk into the immense silence of a regional particular, westerners will still try to rent a soft bed in the hotel of radical innocence. No time for foreplay in the frontier. Lie down and dream of Egypt, due west, a threshold that can never be crossed.

From the outside, the west is a horizon that evokes a character cliché, a feat of cultural engineering.

And the west of westerns – horses and cowboys and ranches and settlers and the shaggy stare of buffalo – incites strange questions.

"A saskatoon?"

Look up "saskatoon" in *The Canadian Encyclopedia*, where one is referred to "Berries, Wild," which follows "Berries, Cultivated," and which proclaim themselves as one of the more than 200 species of berries that grow in Canada, of which only a handful populate the west, and only a further handful are edible. Saskatoon berries, *Amelanchier alnifolia,* are members of the rose family, saskatoon the Cree word for those berries which subsequently migrated to christen the city of Saskatoon east of the western edge of Calgary. These berries were essential to Indians and settlers alike, a major constituent of pemmican, their branches laden every end of July and beginning of August, fruit dropping its plenty into the mouths of bears and children. Even now new varieties of saskatoon are being developed for commercial production, and a persistent westerner can identify a saskatoon bush without hesitation. Every prairie child has been sent off with a bucket and with instructions to come back when that bucket was filled.

Unlikely questions:

"Is it possible to shoot a saskatoon or is that animal too elusive for bullets?"

Here is the perfect metaphor for the west. Shooting a saskatoon. A berry so perfect in its vitamin content, so flavourful, so eloquent with colour at summer's height.

Shooting a saskatoon.

Complex bargaining takes place when westerners blunder beyond their shelterbelts. The myth is a lie and a whopper, westerners have been taken for a ride and a promise, not to mention a prayer.

For all that the west has been so neatly packaged, there are reasons for suspicion. A region wrapped up by the bonds of its own hesitation on a threshold that can't be framed, the west blunders beyond its appropriate edges.

"Can a saskatoon be lassoed?"

One of the ways the west survives is by riding a climax of contemplation. The intricate loop of the chuckwagon races is just such a trope, a contemporary variation on an old refrain. Chuckwagon is a word all westerners know and understand, a wagon fitted with cooking equipment and provisions for cowboys and harvest hands, which follows those riders to their workplace and cooks and feeds them right on the dismounted spot. Chuckwagons are cross-gender, movable sites, both male and female, cookery in a rush, stoves on the run, undomesticated and full of hurrying hunger, but willing to pull up and unhitch, start a fire and settle for grub cooked the old-fashioned way, in a cast iron pot slung from a tripod, in a sizzling frying pan. Chuckwagon races require the knot of a figure eight around two barrels, a rush to the finish. Originally, after the race, an outrider had to start a stove, smoke serving as the sign of arrival, a winner. The chuckwagon races today have omitted that feminine gesture and settled for the sound and fury of horses, neck on neck, thundering across the finish line to the screams of an enthralled crowd.

The Alberta writer Robert Kroetsch: "I thought the sun had given up chuckwagon racing." But there is no escape. The chariots of iconicity are implacable, the phalanx of frontier an invented race around a border of time, chasing history.

Chuckwagon horses wild for speed, thoroughbreds with a history of refusing to obey and thus first rescued from the cannery and then sentenced to a lesser form of racing, harnessed to a chase and a wagon with a strong-armed version of westerner holding the reins, mad to circle the track. When the horn goes, outriders scramble for their saddles. After holding their horses and untangling the reins and tossing in the stove, after trying to mount in that melee of dust and disaster, they too trace the ancient figure eight before racing to catch up to the already speeding wagons. The wagons, wheels and canvas and creaking boxes, pull themselves through that terrible knot around two barrels that must stay upright in their chalk circles while the hooves thundering past could blow them over with sheer velocity. The wagon wheels scream against their axle-grease, and yet, this is an orderly race, no brawl.

No fewer than 37 different infractions and penalties: knocking one of those damn barrels over; wagon interference; outriders failing to follow the proper figure eight; failure to cooperate with the starter; whipping with the ends of lines. Other penalties: falling off your wagon, killing your horses, calling for help, grabbing a thunderbolt, pretending to win, believing in speed, trying to catch time, just plain imagining that you might begin to be able to imagine the west, or any west at all.

That intricate looped pattern a knot that pulls tightness toward incomplete completion, a souvenir and an invention, a carnival that refuses to fold up and close itself down. Stampede, and westerners its celebrants.

The grand myths are crumbling, epics preparing to abandon the west's terrible space. Westerners, eager to blunder beyond improbable seductions, know their west will continue to sneak into midnight dreams, into cloistered gardens, into the sigh of melancholia. These are the gestures of a kitchen, a clothesline, a windbreak, a garden. Without a dream over the next rise, without a horse to mane the wind, without the sad justice of weather, the west holds its breath and waits for the next round of optimists to try and pin it down.

After the railway tracks have been torn up, after the sun has dipped below the towers, after the rivers have conceded to the glaciers' retreat, the west will still be the west, mysterious, unreal, beyond corroboration.

> Some people go to heaven.
> Some people write poems.
> Some people go west
> to homestead.

The words of Robert Kroetsch, a compass.

Forget the homestead. Or the territory. Don't try to predict voting patterns. Remember to walk into the wind, remember to remember the strange creatures living beyond the edge of the world: the wild and untameable saskatoon.

Westerners have no choice but to send our silence and cunning and exile east, shooting saskatoons in Europe, tying ourselves into knots of translation, dying without explaining the westness of west, its nectar taste, its sage smell. Someone, somewhere, whispers in another ear, "go west," and another state of mind stumbles to its feet and tries to untie the intricate knot of language that ties us all to death.

It is easier to shoot a saskatoon than to name this awesomely confounding, unlimited and undefinable space, the westness of west.

Aritha van Herk is the author of five novels: *Judith, The Tent Peg, No Fixed Address* (nominated for the Governor General's Award for fiction), *Places Far From Ellesmere* (a geografictione) and *Restlessness*. Her wide-ranging critical work is collected in *A Frozen Tongue* and *In Visible Ink*; she has published hundreds of articles, reviews and essays. Her irreverent but relevant history of Alberta, *Mavericks: An Incorrigible History of Alberta,* won the Grant MacEwan Author's Award for Alberta Writing and frames the Mavericks exhibition at the Glenbow Museum and Archives in Calgary. With George Webber she has published *In This Place: Calgary 2004-2011* (Photographs by George Webber, Words by Aritha van Herk) and most recently, *Prairie Gothic.* She teaches Creative Writing and Canadian Literature at the University of Calgary in Calgary. She is a Fellow of the Royal Society of Canada, a member of the Alberta Order of Excellence, recipient of the Lorne Pierce Medal and the Lieutenant Governor's Distinguished Artist Award.